VIPER JAZZ

The Wesleyan Poetry Program: Volume 82

JAMES TATE

MIDDLETOWN, CONNECTICUT

VIPER JAZZ

WESLEYAN UNIVERSITY PRESS

811
T

Acknowledgement is gratefully made to the following periodicals, in the pages of which most of the poems in this book were first published: *Aldebaran, The Antioch Review, Apocalypse, Arion's Dolphin, The Ark River Review, The Chicago Tribune Magazine, The Dickinson Review, Epoch, Fire Exit, Granite, The Iowa Review, Jeopardy, kayak, Lillabulero, Lotus, The Massachusetts Review, The New Boston Review, New Letters, The Ohio Review, Paintbrush, Poetry Now, The Shore Review, Some,* and *Transatlantic Review.* Acknowledgement is also made to Bellevue Press, Rook Press, and the University of Connecticut Library, the original publishers of three of the poems in this book on broadsides.

Library of Congress Cataloging in Publication Data

Tate, James, 1943–
    Viper jazz.

    (The Wesleyan poetry program: v. 82)
    I. Title.
PS3570.A8V5   811'.5'4   76–4943
ISBN 0-8195-2082-9
ISBN 0-8195-1082-3 pbk.

Manufactured in the United States of America
First edition

FOR LISELOTTE

CONTENTS

VIPER JAZZ

POEM (I Can't Speak for the Wind)

I don't know about the cold.
I am sad without hands.
I can't speak for the wind
which chips away at me.
When pulling a potato, I see only the blue haze.
When riding an escalator, I expect something orthopedic
      to happen.
Sinking in quicksand, I'm a wild appaloosa.
I fly into a rage at the sight of a double-decker bus,
I want to eat my way through the Congo,
I'm a double-agent who tortures himself
and still will not speak.
I don't know about the cold,
But I know what I like I like a tropical madness,
I like to shake the coconuts
and fingerprint the pythons, —
fevers which make the children dance.
I am sad without hands,
I'm very sad without sleeves or pockets.
Winter is coming to this city,
I can't speak for the wind
which chips away at me.

SCHIZOPHRENIC KISS

And what a day it was!
This was the night we had been
in the jungle as well as in the city:
It was night everywhere,
with spiderbones beneath the costume in the cellar
and still no fountain of ink.
The suburbs as well,
what we could see of them.
Their personalities and pasts to a certain extent
are the most ancient and sacred:
when we finally decided to take the subway
with a tape-recorder for our summerhouse.
And during the days, what there was of them,
a little monkey woke me.
It was light enough to read
the handwriting of someone
who appeared to not care,
and stumble without regard
to collect the birds from apple trees
on secret hands and knees
night after night after.

SENSITIVE EARS

It's a tiny noise
like that of eyeliner being applied
like a twenty-year-old smell coming back
to haunt you in a dream
it's the new house
it must be the old house
only this time it enters
through the ears
what a strange odor!
like an entire New Year's Eve Party
shoved down a laundry chute
like waking up from an automobile accident
twenty years older!
and I keep sleeping in the basement
to get away from it
I'm in the treetops
listening to it circle
and I hear a mule puff its last sigh
I can't shut off this wheezing
there's a noise crouched under that leaf
I'm a flea with a thousand microphones
for eyes.

CRUISIN' EVEN

In order to belong to the Million Mile
Club one must belong to the Society
to Prevent Intelligent Intercourse.
The spirit is said to escape, especially

in crowds, like a shout in the park.
First there is an oral examination:
such questions as: Can we just sit here
in silence without resort to meditation?

What is the secret meaning of "organic"?
Does everything change at the same rate?
Is the typewriter organic? At one point,
a brain-damaged highschool poetry teacher

says, "Fantastic, look at that moon Marie!"
Sitting on a sponge, practicing for the
unknown. It will go away tomorrow, he
thinks to himself, lost in long, hollow

tunnels of night-thought. A longwinded
novel about a man who thinks he is reading
a longwinded novel. "What is the other me
doing right now who is not reading this?"

Silence for forty pages. Comfort in knowing
that you belong to a chain-gang of such
wretches, from where this mobile of a life
appears to stand perfectly still.

America, kiss my ass! I didn't mean that,
laughing myself sideways down the cul-
de-sac and into the Franz Kafka Re-election
Committee headquarters: Prague comes

to Prairie Village, a rather cuddly ghost,
still miraculously unweary of understanding
the speakable sadness of a dried-up port.

EAVESDROPPER WITHOUT A PORT, BECOMING SMALL

Arabs are twisting downshore,
members of a leading desert tribe.
Perhaps they have lost contact
with their highschool peers,
lovers, golfers and fishermen.

Waves can be as formless: over
illuminations, cocktail nuts drift.
The Captain in his bathtub tells
terrible stories, false stories
of breathless beginnings in a shivery cove,
which turn out to be the same as this one
by a thick thread of broken paddles.

The fabulous highwayman considers remaining
on this island never adequately explained,
without regard to time, space or spectators.
And by rubbing granite cliffs together
morning becomes Thor Heyerdahl
on his way to work: a cannon announces
spring groping its way
as a hearse among lotus blossoms.

The zebras want to visit Chicago:
it is said they have memories but they don't.
They receive their energies
from a completely unknown source,
some malignant force is directing them.
The electricity from our nightmares?
Full of illusory weathervanes and silent cocks
that sleep past noon, in a field of marble?

16

FOR PEKKA, FOR JORMA

I'm not even thanked
for the pairs of ancient socks
I leave everywhere;
and I'm continually forgotten
for the holes I'm always leaving
in the rivers of blood
that are meant to be drunk
and not sailed on.

Dear Comrades,
the duck walked across the lake.
I am still in love with Marfa.
We have no plans.
She has a nipple on her eyeball.
Hours go by with nothing but
the refreshing, occasional doubt
if we still exist.
Quite understandable.
I believe me, go ahead,
I believe anything.
I know another
has a nail in his soul.

But at least without legs
I'm cured of my fear of falling—
all the way from the soles of my shoes
to the dust of the earth;
falling from my fingertips
into the eyes of one last moment
before I must say goodbye
to the soothsayers of Lahti,
to the fishermen who use their hearts as bait.

A VOYAGE FROM STOCKHOLM
TO TAKE ADVANTAGE OF LOWER PRICES
ON THE FINNISH ISLAND OF ÅLAND

Out through the frosty archipelago
card-players, morning beer-drinkers,
parsimonious housewives
and Nick Carter readers:

the derelict bum
seems to have a universe
of oddities folded, wrapped, stashed
in his filthy bag:
his tireless attention
to a thousand scraps of paper.

Someone hums a love song
while the others sleep.
No matter how far he might travel
his secret story is written somewhere,
in the generous air, in the distance.

A little patch of sky between suburbs,
about the size of a football field,
or maybe it's a dusty parkinglot,
sees him waving, and is reminded of; —
and in the distance the distance . . .

THE HAIRY CUP OF COFFEE

I was the good guy in *Revenge of the Amoebas*.
You missed it? Too bad: the reviews said
"Loaded toothpaste!" "Revolutionary toothpaste!"

The last scene, where I'm caught drinking
the hairy cup of coffee, and say
to the psychosomatic waiter:

"How much for the dog and the car?
How much for the chair and the piece of cheese?
How much for the cat and the glass of wine?
How much for the rock and the airplane?"

"Depending on the influence
the napkin had on your life, Sir!"
Who could trust a man like that, with a face

you might find on a coughdrop box?
As I made to go, strawberry flames licking
my white knee, he delicately pinpricked

my pinprick.

ALFONSO LACKLUSTRE

The shoe was occupied, kind of a picnic
rented to another living companion.
An excellent raincoat makes the bed.
The belt is not heavy, no heavier than the old man's
sleepy lecture on a handkerchief.
It's already 8 o'clock and she is full.
Her driver's license is only moonshine.
She is comfortable with a difficult word.

Is it kind to be amusing, healthy to be striped?
This is my everyday room, full of trays.
The floorlamps are also fruitbowls.
I can boil coffee on the ceiling.
There is a small, three-legged bench in the corner.
Simple and wild this new pillow.
Yesterday morning, tomorrow morning
are immigrants with one shirt between them.

He has a broken foot and has employed a cane
to stop the bus. Later, he'll use his tie
to stir coffee, proof that one has
sufficient money to enter the town.

In back of the bridge chewing-gum
is permitted to work, hair is slicked back
in church. To believe. To live. To feel.
To sew. To dress. To row. To plant.
To shoe a horse. To tell the future.
To flee! Sure. Certainly. Is there
any sleeper on the train? When is
the next train leaving. I'll take that.
I would like a ballpoint pen.
I would like a postcard.

So sad that she is sick!
I dial the right number I dial the wrong number.
She puts down the receiver she picks it up.
That's all right where's the wastebasket,
when does the game begin,
where can I find a small shop selling chocolates?

LIAISONS

He was obviously the emissary
and we shook hands with the secret shake.
He was not surprised by me
nor I by him.

"I made use of your absence to remember you,"
doffing his cap cordially.

Why did I let him speak to me
those warm rivers.
Children in wheelchairs came down the hill.

"I made use of your absence to remember you,"
he repeated cruelly.

TWO FOR THE SAVANT OF MOUNTAIN ROAD

1. *The Sky*

What is the sky?
A week later
I reply: I don't know,

why don't you ask
your only friend.
Another week passes.
He doesn't call.

He must be up to something,
he must know
what the hell it is.

I look at my bankbook,
it's forty-seven below.
Can you give me a clue?

I blurt at him.
Those few shining masterpieces
are lost, electric piercing

bouquets
lost in a fantastic fire.
What is the sky?

What is the sky.
The sky is a door,
a very small door

that opens for an inchworm
an inch above his rock,
and keeps his heart from flying off.

   2. *Nothing*

It is a tiny obscure lighthouse
for serious travellers of the night
whose only vocation
is to gradually discover a spot
to root their lonely wardrobes.

It is a dignified fifth-columnist
inspiring unheard-of wind
slightly ajar:
if you haven't got any you'll die.

It's not going to improve your posture.
Take an overdose and you won't even faint.
It helps you make it through the day.
You can take it with you and that's all.

LATER THE SAME MINUTE

Well I certainly don't remember that.
My goals were changing
and I didn't know it.
Estimates of the dislocation are not in yet.
Due to the distance of television
some states were affected,
no one speaks of their unknown histories,
what so-and-so said at an earlier time.
It was very close to each of us,
we felt like moonmen falling in love,
refusing the next trip back
because . . . grievous radiolarians,
because . . . pensive ibises . . .
to avoid dark bananas:

The President was reminded of the story
of Adolphe Sax who as a boy
in early 19th-century Belgium
was struck on the head by a brick.
The accident-prone lad also swallowed a needle,
fell down a flight of stairs,
toppled onto a burning stove,
and accidently drank some sulphuric acid.

When he grew up he invented the saxophone.

AWKWARD SILENCE

The trees are sprayed
to give the birds
a slight shock
to avoid unwanted attacks
on the President.

Who was it that first started counting,
the first looter?
the one who stripped the dead
of their souvenirs?

We are breaking through so many illusions,
like some kind of ghost dance!
Nothing passes unmarked,
even the machines gossip.

Two powder puffs are talking
on the veranda
while helicopters mate overhead.
The laboratory of eternal sleep

tied to a cat's tail
suffers the little children to suffer.
A ruined church, a ruined library, —
a hospital wishes it were dead.

The room is bugged,
it sucks off energy.
I don't care for its windows anymore,
as if this piece of earth had the right,

to tear up the darkness in search of night.
It's the days when nothing happens,
not a word is spoken,
those are the ones that can be saved.

THE DOOR

I try to keep in mind
that you can always
walk out the door,

the door, the door, the door.

what does *dore* mean
dore doesnt mean anything.
well then what does *doar* mean
doesn't doesn't mean anything to me either.
What about *dour*.
I think it means something.
I'm waking up.

RICH FRIENDS, POOR FRIENDS

Humans slaughtered by gossip
and the Cokes were far, far away.
How's one to live? Can't
wander forever inspired by
tasty dinners: "Is my seatbelt
fastened, Gloria?"
He pummels the countryside
with tiny vodka empties,
thinking: "With a wife
like mine, fuck ecology."
Met Hedy Lamarr drunk.
No bananas, she announced.
Blah fuck my dog blah
rover over with a lawnmower.
Things get handed down
and nothing changes but death
and taxes. I made a deal
with my son: If I'd let my hair
grow down to my shoulders,
he'd get a crewcut.
Can you name the highest mountain
in Virginia? If he'd promise
not to kill me, I'd
teach him how to murder.

A RADICAL DEPARTURE

Bye!

I'm going to a place so thoroughly remote
you'll never hear from me again.

No train ship plane or automobile
has ever pierced its interior

I'm not even certain it's still there
or ever was
the maps are very vague about it
some say here some say there
but most have let the matter drop

Yes of course it requires courage
I'll need two bottles of vintage champagne every day
to keep the morale high

and do you mind if I take your wife?
Well, I guess this is it
we'll see ourselves to the door

Where are we . . . ?

COME THE THAW

There is a conspiracy
for and against you:
a nebulous precision
like the feel of suicide,
worlds refused by worlds.

Your far-juggled head
whines, then dines on the rot,
a ghost among the living,
no color and gentle tossing
nightmare: quick, up

with the nets and anchor
before we attacked
by the big fish!
I hope it's not in our building,
right up to the end.

THE TELEVISION WAS REMINDED OF THE STORY

This was before the first test pattern.

One night Slim Victuals, Estil Loney and
Snörpa Little-Dew were out on a spree—

apricot-juice heads all.
They knocked over a couple of tabularasas.

Snörpa whispered
into the ear of a passing shoplifter:
"You have just made a complete fool of yourself!"

This is not that kind of town,
they told themselves:
this is our home, the town of stove-pipe hats.

A sign said YIELD
and a woman ran through the streets
actually crying.

MANY PROBLEMS

In a flophouse
a man has it out
with his obsessions:
he's locked up in a room with them
for a whole night, what the hell
make it a lifetime.
He's scratched that wall so long
it's a solid chalk-white.

Meanwhile, the ceiling's caving in,
and somebody's ceiling
is his floor.
The waterheater's gone mad,
boiling water from every tap
including the toilet.
It breaks the mug.

Besides that he's locked in.
The whole building
is tilting that way
and then this, like a tower of spaghetti.
Imagining that it's his dinner
causing all this fickle equilibrium,
the loss of it,
when actually
it's the boneyard of vegetables
the whole world is built on,
or the stupid meatball in question.

A BOX FOR TOM

These exquisite rags carry
the lice of history.
They've been there,
great cities turning in the night,
lamplit barges haunting
industrious rivers,
weepy adieus at a farm
on the edge of a prairie.

Here are worthy garments
to be worn as camouflage
for your lofty character,
to hide your misfit spirit;
fit for slumming in some
of the very best restaurants,
at home with snobs who snub you,
and generally causing a stir
among birds of flight and terrapins.

You can retrace an old ghost's
bad luck back to the pot of gold
in a poolhall getting a start
then missing, falling, staining
everything to match his shoes
which were covered with doglime,
angel hair and bad news.

READ THE GREAT POETS

What good is life without music.
But that's impossible,
one shuffle has always led to another.
One man hears it start on his lathe,
a mother beats her eggs.
There's a typewriter in the next room.
Two cars are angry at each other.
The baby downstairs is wet again.
I remember the voice of a dead friend.
Everything speaks at the same time.
Music will watch us drown.

I write letters to all those from whom I receive
and to many of those from whom I don't.
I read books, anything, useless piles of random
insufferable rubbish for which, in my torpid panic,
I fall through time and space each day
in my foolish way, remembering only the present feeling,
not the village with its face of death,
nothing to be carried secretly in a car.
I move from the stiff-backed chair
to the brown leather one
as the day wears on. And then finally
the couch, allowing the spirit to leave
the broken body and wander at will.
Lately it's a pasture of Holsteins she longs for.

There's a certain point in each evening when I have to put on some really soul-shattering rock-and-roll music and comb my hair into this special caveman fright-wig. I've done as much as two or even three dollars worth of damage to my apartment in one hour of all-stops-pulled Bacchic, Dionysian celebration and revolution of this great dull life, so fascinating it hypnotizes you and then puts you to sleep, only to never know the ending. It's strange though, no one ever complains. Is it what I feared all along? We are playing the same song and no one has ever heard anything.

People read poems like newspapers, look at paintings as though they were excavations in the City Center, listen to music as if it were rush hour condensed. They don't even know who's invaded whom, what's going to be built there (when, if ever). They get home. That's all that matters to them. They get home. They get home alive.

So what it's been burgled. The heirlooms. Mother's rings, father's cufflinks. They go to a distant island and get robbed there. It's the same everywhere. Read the great poets, listen to the great composers. It's the same everywhere. The Masters. The Thieves.

ON THE SUBJECT OF DOCTORS

I like to see doctors cough.
What kind of human being
would grab all your money
just when you're down?
I'm not saying they enjoy this:
"Sorry, Mr. Rodriguez, that's it,
no hope! You might as well
hand over your wallet." Hell no,
they'd rather be playing golf
and swapping jokes about our feet.

Some of them smoke marijuana
and are alcoholics, and their moral
turpitude is famous: who gets to see
most sex organs in the world? Not
poets. With the hours they keep
they need the drugs more than anyone.
Germ city, there's no hope
looking down those fire-engine throats.
They're bound to get sick themselves
sometime; and I happen to be there
myself in a high fever
taking my plastic medicine seriously
with the doctors, who are dying.

BLANK-STARE ENCOUNTER

I met a blank stare on the street. That could be me in there trying to claw myself out. I leaned up against its stomach: different accent altogether. I was understandably discouraged and threw up; thought virtue was a dump on the head. After all, he can offer the excuse that he was in a hurry. What a sight he was! He broke off a branch and threw his keys away, all with the blankest stare, in Paris, on the Rue rue, on the night of the Raving Madonna, in my eye, O incarnadine: He was the leader of several tragic movements, an abominable mirrorman spotlighting the hushful sockets. Sometimes I felt very recherché around him, sometimes inclined to chaperon. The blank stare: his podiatrist thinks he ought to be in the movies. He is also considering the Marching Baton Squadron. I bite my knuckles with sudden inexplicable passion! I want to start a new religion, on the spot, but the blank stare drags me along, a terrible dragon snapping at the moon. His blank stare must have been very painful. He opened his mouth once to let out a dead rat.

SAME TITS

It was one of those days. I was walking down the St. and this poster glassed in a theater billboard caught my eye. A really gorgeous set of tits. It was noon, hot as hell outside. So I said what the hell, paid my $2.50 and went in. Got a seat all by myself right in the middle. The curtain opens: there's the same poster by itself in the middle of the stage. I sat there sweating. Finally decided to get the hell out of there. It was still noon, hot as hell outside.

HOOKED ON A STAR

I like everything about you
though you are just a piece of plastic,
I know that and it doesn't influence me.
I still love you.

We can spend the night in my room.
The room doesn't stink.
I am beginning to smell for the first time.
It's always the first time.

I won't even speak about your singing.
You have a voice like red ants.

ONCE I WAS YOUNG IN THE LAND OF BALONEY

It is boring to watch an old peacock
achieve his end on the cactus-creeping hills.
I want baloney, he cries.

A simpering reporter steps out
of a big, gray boulder and says:
" 'scuse me, Old Boy, but could you tell me
the difference between the idea and
the execution? "
                    —I gotcha!

Well, this is certainly a feast, baloney
everywhere. Baloney squashed into my doll's fangs,
baloney baloney and to a certain extent chance
needed and yes even deserved all this baloney,

the ghost of baloney through violent will
toothless wrenching baloney now you are still.

POWER OF YOUTH

I picture myself as a hummingbird
or as a nail robbing a grave.
I drink wind from the skull by candlelight.
I can catch rabbits
or fish between my teeth.
My friend levitates and people
throw cups of hot coffee
in their own faces.

Only black magic left in the Vatican.
I know his name.

THE LADDER DOWN

I touched her with my cigarette,
"It feels cool."
I stuck her with a pin,
"A feather, it tickles me."

A fish kissed her and orgasm:
she was only two weeks old,
she could see the wallpaper,
feel the crib.

Into her grave with one more
sentence, I always knew
something terrible
was going to happen.

PARENTAL GUIDANCE

Gee whiz another
gin fizz:
O Mother, please
let me go to the drug addicts'
ball tonight.
Father, may I borrow the .38
if I promise not to be home late?
Yes I know how to use it
get yourself hard in the bathroom
and gently roll it on.
If you want to throw up
stick it down your throat,
shoot the lights out
and ask Margie to go steady
car wreck, jail and geometry.

LOVE

I only need it once a year
and then for just a minute.
It's my birthday and that's
why I call it my deathday.
I've never gotten very good at
it, I forget to remember.

I want something very strange
to happen: *She is everywhere
at once*! Each room is swallowed
by the tireless hands of the
blind, the brilliant tropical
colors throb up the long trembling
fingers . . . But I don't know anything,
I can't remember. I only
need it once a year and then
for just a minute.

WHO GETS THE BITTERROOT?

Dr. Bitterroot was called out on a housecall,
leaving his pipe aglow in the hands of his wife, Mrs.
    Bitterroot.
Down the flowing waters of the Bitterroot River
floated Dr. Kenneth Bitterroot in his brand new
Bitterroot outboard toward the ailing lady's
aching side. Dr. Bitterroot right away
diagnosed a rotten cancerous bitterroot
and reached for his bitterroot which he stabbed
into her bitterroot up the bitterroot canal.

Her husband, a bitterroot farmer, looked on.
Dr. Bitterroot sewed her up quickly
and said to the disconsolate farmer:
"There, she's all yours; good as new,
but no bitterroot and no bitterroot cancer."
The farmer walked into the kitchen scratching his head
which was slowly growing another bitterroot.
"Dr. Bitterroot," he said, "I don't suppose
you'll be needing that bitterroot."

"I need this bitterroot to get home," said Dr. Bitterroot.
"Mrs. Bitterroot always likes to know where I've been."

43

DREAM OF A PROSE POEM

Pssst! Over here! Over here, over here, dummy.
I can't see you. Now can you see me? What do you want?
It's nice here. We like it a lot, don't we, sweetie?
No, I don't. It's a real-estate firm, not very big,
not long, but still. Are you all right? When I was fiddling . . .
Yes, yes, I'm fine; just concentrating on driving. Pssst.
Over here. The Lovely New Miss Cancer was gently sobbing
into a nosegay of violets as though to a glacial music.
The space she had occupied before now glowed like a neon
doorway. We're here, I think. We thought you weren't
coming. But then, said the male egg, a silversmith
from White Russia, you won't have something to drink?
Some kind of egg opera was petering to its climax.
We like the privacy here we've found milk to be cheaper
at the . . . Of course the post is slower. These new
day-glo cerements they're selling over at Fosterson's,
it's a fad. Were you ever in Lone Tree, Missouri?
I sold you the newspaper, mascara running horribly.
But why did you ask? How did you know?

A LETTER TO DATA SERVICE

Yesterday, rebuffed by a sewer,
and humming while running
through woods
from estranged animals,
I ran into a house of cards
and called it poesie.
I turned up the music to
98.6°,
arranged for a barbecue
for and of diplomats,
so distant were friends
that dry, grey afternoon.
The library cried,
I dreamed of an empty room
locked for some twenty-nine years.
How I hated the blank pages!

Data Service, I owe you my days.
There may be shades, but there is
a monolithic thrust
to the general sameness.
I'm a mad passive, the crimes seem
so evenly distributed.
I hope something arrives before
you receive this so I can feel
guilty for writing.

"I KNOW SOMEONE FROM ANOTHER WORLD"

I know someone from another world is trying to get through to me, a righteous bum travelling exclusively by UFOs. I rip at the air to make room for myself; I jump through the hole I've ripped in the air. I sit down now in my positively evil matchbox: but I don't do that too quickly. First I wave my arms around like two suffering, mad pitchforks. I stick carrots in my ears, dirty socks down my throat, and splash globs of rubber glue into my eyeballs. I have never seen this positively evil matchbox before. Oh how I love this positively evil matchbox! Nothing tastes good in here!

Sounds like somebody's great symphony played backwards on a block of ice with an icepick! Dear colleagues, never wake from your dream — it's so malignantly dull! so *so what* ! Who is this traveller? Who is calling? I sit down now in my positively evil matchbox, in the church of my childhood one last time. I'll need presents wherever I go from now on.

THE POOR REACH

Now when I address you
it is somebody else speaking.
I couldn't be in two places at once,
could I?
You sound like a real fruitcake man.
You're going to drive me to Mattapan!
I'll put on my boots of adventure,
my little nookie of robots.
I stand outside the dark;
I am the first there
to pick up the change.
Poor Trotsky. Well, he lives
in the movies, in the donutholes . . .

MY FIRST BLOOMERS

Jokes are for the living
the dead know everything

I can't think of any good ones
then think of the grass on their graves

I am riding on the edge of Spring
I feel my beautiful suicides

My first bloomers . . .

47

TO WASTE

I fold the blanket of years into one soft triangle
of blue

MURDER STORY

Grisly leaves used to be attracted
to meatwrappers that blew across
downtown streetcorners in the Midwest
on the first winter night in November.

Sassafras and cinnamon toast,
gingerbread and hot chocolate,
milktoast and pumpkin pie —
the rest is like a symphony
through which one fell.

The Thanksgiving police say
"To hell with Buddha!"
The milkman won't tell his story.
Get up and change the people

will ya stupor man.

48

VALUE

There they go, the workers, the saints
of the hubcap and all that. These are the actual
workers who make all our necessary items.

Inside the factory the foreman is sleeping in a corner.
His coffee is cold and sunlight refracts on his pate.
The workers gawk at him, then get an idea:
stick matches under his lids and light them.

Upstairs men roll up their sleeves
and smoke long daydream cigars.
At the end of the day a little baby
is handed to the king.
He turns it over in his hand and says:

"Throw it away; it stinks."

PATTERNS FADE

Each man is held responsible
for keeping one force in check:
Bob watches a certain virus,
he pulls the alarm the minute
one of them tries to escape.

And as he turns to pull the alarm,
another leaves by the back exit.
But his conscience is clear because
now it is another man's problem.

Dave discovers a new virus
with mixed emotions: Sure, it will
make his career, but what might it do
to the human race. That is
another man's problem, who calculates

that, at this rate, we have proven
ourselves to be great runners,
perhaps too fast. Some say
we have a hundred years at best.

Some say our problem is the sun,
there's nothing we can do,
it is burning itself up.
Then famine, bombs and man's
indigestible hatred of himself.

Each man is thinking to himself:
"I'm not doing my job, I'm causing
the whole race to perish,
my indifference, my selfishness."

No one dies this time though
they sit very, very still.

THE GENTLE BECKENDORFS

They are all living in a commune now
in Xenia, Ohio. It is called
The Gentle Beckendorfs' Commune
and anyone can join
for one hundred thousand dollars.

But you have to gather your own yams;
and everytime you hurt somebody's feelings
it costs you another thousand dollars.

Before long you realize you are a slave
to all this gentleness;
but then you go broke
and their love mysteriously lingers.

You're the tiny thing they carry
inside of themselves wherever they go.

DRY CUP

And you my cone
of hot nickels
my pietà
with a steaming locomotive

problem child

The pyrotechniques
that bring you back
in the sad form
in the formless sandbox

without shores

where you're drowning
to hold up your feet
you're dying to show us
something really wet

and shining

with your sideburns lit up
to show us the meaning
what a flivver
what a brief cameo

ad for pain.

The architecture, sleepy Mexican,
is afraid to go out.
Young couples go there to settle down
and not raise a family.
Retired people open shops
and refuse to sell anything.
It is an easy place to like
without really liking it.
You can get to know
without really knowing it.
It's the invisible that is ruthless.
Somebody is going to grow up
and kill it, make a killing,
so you'll never seem so lonesome.

MARFA

I sent my love to the showers.
My sisters are on the blink.
The beer must take a letter.
These poems are on the house.
Say you miss me, Marf, I'm out of gas.
If this is the information you've been seeking,
I'm a lost and pissed-off alias.
My personal self has not felt your private breasts.
I mean nothing to the circles of mocha.
I was not born there.

I'm consoled by this hole
where you once tarried, a rope
around the wilderness.
You've got me surrounded.
I can't come any closer.
I crawl inside you like a car.

Is it true that we are fools
to have ever expected
anything else?
Just once we should have been
staring at one another
over candlelight and cognac
in a Grand Hotel anywhere.
Two people can build one fast
in emergency situations
which have been the only ones
dealt us thus far.
But we couldn't even afford the poverty.

Marfa, I'm still locked up in jail
with boxcars on my mind.
Marfa, today I'm so happy all this is falling apart.
I give my purse strings a tug
and drive on through the grove.
Saw my hand shrivel.
Saw rags swim across the sky.
I dreamed I was home, and that I had left,
I had even left the leaving, so far back was this
I was supposed to be home thirty years ago.
My wife will think I don't love her.
My beautiful wife!
Or was it my mother?

You've gone walking on the mountain alone.
There was much sadness in your face.
I've hurt you again over the price of cheese.
Without you, the calm is delirious.
Perhaps up there you can look down on me and laugh.
Marfa has nothing, she is pure spirit up there.
(I could say something nice about her now that she is gone:
She has perfect teeth. And not only that
                              she rules the world.)

                    Wall of death edumacation
                         booky booky
                    manic blue flowers
                              for
                         Marfa
                         silver flowers
                         silver flowers for Marfa
                         the wall of death
                         stack my deck
                         for Marfa
                    Manic blue flowers.

BLONDE BOMBSHELL UNNERVES SQUIRTS

She is between a train and a cloud.
The train thinks about this
and flies into a rage
across Niagara Falls,
eating the barrels of thin mystics,
spitting them out like stars,
like welts on a pig.
She is eating a little bitty cow, full of rain.
After all, why was she standing there
if only to be as pugnacious as possible.
Perhaps she is going to meet someone —
a dashing captain, her dead mother, some local squirts.
Now she is walking away from the cloud, yes,
she is walking away from the train also.

VIOLET

Smothered in camouflage of hangdog shy her tiny limp
thunder

AMHERST TO EASTHAMPTON

I ain't got no body
seizing my spirit.
My spiritual body has no body.
My body has no body,
and my spirit hath no spirit.
like the like the like the like the
nest of spiders beneath your arms,
the wind carries your shadow through her dark hills.

The darkness you cast off seeks me,
eats a hole through the chocolate forest that separates us,
empty spaces filled with a fine down.

HONEYMOON

We were making love in a speedboat
firing a real cannonball over the lake.
We really should have been communing
with Ibsen's ghost, announced by an
excellent Hungarian waiter and drinking
straight tequila in the Ozarks.
It should have been the time of our lives
in Helsinki, I wanted to make it all worth while.
Perhaps an Irish setter by the fireplace
thrown in to prove I am at peace with you
anywhere. Our favorite song came on
the radio as we hung on to the last
noodle of consciousness. Instead,
found ourselves bouncing checks and
terrified by the bridges, without food
or rest, or gas for that matter. We should
have been rushing for cocktails smack
into the Berlin Wall, instead of ourselves.

THE BEAN-SHORTAGE LOOK

What's wrong
with a bouillon cube
for two?
Don't tell me
you dropped
the apartment key
down the elevator shaft
again; I can't stand it.
I guess we'd better cancel
the trip. I don't know
if I've had a heart attack
or a nervous breakdown
but the sky has opened up
and I think I am going
to disappear forever.
Hold my hand!
I'm afraid to close my eyes!
Do you recognize me?

THE GLASSY HARBOR

O faint sad noises
and milky dullness,

rose-colored blindness
in evening gowns

how moist and rhythmic
those who walk near

the glassy harbor.
Silent drift of deserters

from the theater,
and everywhere the stars

receding, receding . . .
nothing to hold onto

but their own silver hearts.

"DREAMY CARS GRAZE ON THE DEWY BOULEVARD"

Dreamy cars graze on the dewy boulevard.
Darkness is more of a feeling inside the drivers.
The city is welded together
out of hope and despair.
The seasons pass imperceptibly,
more of a feeling inside the streetcleaners:

"Come quick, Hans,
a leaf is falling inside of me!"

DISEASE

We were just a couple of drifters
on this planet of
some odd billion customers
open all night. She was always
loving and attentive
but made
what I considered
an abnormal number of morbid references,
so that at times I felt like a fungus.
Meanwhile, we drank and smoked
and listened to country music.
She died in her room
and I died in mine.

RETURN

I know, I give you no choice
with my presence about you
hanging like smoke rings, but

why must you exhaust me with
your indefatigable beauty;
I mean, it's there and it's there

and it's always there rocking me
direct into paradise. All right,
let's change the subject.

I live by the photographs of
your motion, we brush cheeks
while changing rooms, the finite

sadness of your profile leads
the way for my transfixion
while I behold your hesitating

approval. That early morning
descent into Amsterdam,
steeples piercing the heavy mist,

and then the hare on the runway . . .
We were that much closer,
you waved a flame over me.

FIRST NIGHT

He's taking down the ladder.
I was just about to say
the roof will never be finished,

because it was perfect
to begin with, in it's shabby silence,
giving me bounce by bounce

the progress of the kingdom of squirrels
with their twitchy problems
and sun-up scramble.

I found that and even the rain
to be a positive boon to the overall
welfare of my spiritual life.

It was the new life. And then,
very suddenly, it was the old life.
(The ladder is gone . . . only a few birds

and a needlepoint of crickets.)
The girl on the horse hasn't returned.
She follows the breathless sheep of demons.

THE THIEF OF SILENCE

You are known by the hermits to be staying here.
I formerly used to live in a certain tree.
Here I come. There I go.
Desirous of seeing, what do you intend to say?
What gain accrues to you by concealing?
Have done with going to the forest
if one goes to heaven by killing animals.

Indicate the place to me where I am to live
for I do not perceive what should drive away my sorrow.
I punish you for that thought
in the evening and morning
with the raw truth of a tiger.

I return to myself
after a thousand million nights of travel.
Who lived here while I was gone?
Did she water the delicate fern?
What did I dream
as I ran down those long, humming streets?
Does anyone remember if I take milk in my tea?
If I knew my name before I departed,
why did I leave
for all the great mountains
and all the forgotten seas?

BUG SLEEP

The bugs' sleep is full of lead,
full of love for the earth.
Sprawled out like body surfers,

dark little angels,

can they hear a tapping on the floor?

And when the bugs' sleep is loosed
at sunrise

it flies into the trees
and perches there
like the shining-back of golden moments.

ONE TRAVELLER TO ANOTHER

See the moonlight on that birch?
The birch accepts it
and feels no need to cry out

Look! I've been touched!

DEPARTURE FOR HUNTING

Isolation now, old tree,
shoulder-leaning buddy,
now we must dream of food —
Rude reminder, I'm coming.

I invented the wheel this morning,
warmed my hands over a fire.
Sacred beast, I'm coming
though future gods haven't been warned.

I hear my hairs growing fine,
I'll have my way.
Love-fury, dandelion, —
Isolation now, old tree!

THE IDIOT

He needed to believe
the wilderness was his aunt
in his solitude:
No one knows we can talk like this, he said.

The path bored him
like an allegory.
A ghostly calm held him in its revelation.
It never occurred to him
to fall down crying.

Dream of a white miner
who steals, part of his radishes.
The icy bicycle stops in the dark
for Spring is in the room, still green.

Trained slugs race across his jello
in eight-cylinder sombreros.
Someone heard his newspaper
nibbling a bush.
The sun hauled up its shaky carriage
and disappeared.

Suddenly refreshed
as though deeper into the darkness of afternoon
relishing the pungent mulch and
swelling with animal desire —
the big game was gone of course
but still there were the birds and squirrels.

WAKE UP

For November it is November,
you were always so proud of that.
It's the first cold day
of a cold day's insistence,

the crisp tautness you've waited for.
There you are, wrapped:
you have good sense, yes,
you've been anxious for something like this.

AUTUMN

The transference bird of little mind has risen high
by its wings of coincidence
in the spacious sphere
of ineffable radiant light
in the lamasery of Pullahari
in the lamasery of non-dual carburetors

In the offering pit of the apparitional body
the fuel of evil tendencies of normal forms
the fuel of dream tendencies
that have been heated up
in the lamasery of the sharp knife
a heavenly tree with which the corpse fans himself.

POEM

Language was almost impossible in those days
as we know it now and then.

When you tell me about your operation
I hear you, but I don't hear you.

Wind gathers behind a barn:
torches are lit, men whisper.

One wears a hat and is very serious
about the war in his bedroom.

"Does it seem like I am sleeping all the time?"
Ask me another question.

Look, Ma, I found something beautiful today
out in the forest, it's still alive . . .

IN A MOTEL ON LAKE ERIE

Tequila & chicken
causing lunar distress.
Nothing promising
on the tb — one symphony
of skeletons, two
black dots, one mountebank
of incurable disease,
one rainbow ground into
dog-ticks. Oh, it is dark here.
I can hear squeaks, probably
elephants. I try to call
the cops but they're
at the ballgame, a benefit
for those who can see.
I turn the lights on in my skull —
what a beautiful evening!
It is like a tombstone
full of vital information.
The highway eagles now
living out this dream.

I SPEAK NO LANGUAGE, I PLAY NO INSTRUMENT

My crumbs are the only ones
in the forest
and still the birds prefer
to make snowbirds in the snow.
I feel like I'm in the same
deserted train station
as those birds, as that snow.

What I need is a chiropractor
for those trees.
I can hear my mother calling,
"Don't touch that snow,
you don't know
where it's been!"

Crumbs down the birds' dry throats.

A DIME FOUND IN THE SNOW

Tomorrow the future will be here,
open her great droopy eye.
She will clean out the barn
with a white boa thrown round her neck
while the pterodactyl dreams
in his floral chambers, destitute
of feathers and the supporting surface
of wings, dreams of the difference
between a long time and a short time,
of getting out of this life
and staying—a flower and a fire engine,
out of this world. Miss Future
might remember something, some summer,

but she's tired and anxious
for a new oblivion, something
to agitate her. Just for the hell of it
she has the ball on the lawn
roll away from home. The opponent,
her father, takes advantage of this
situation, this holiday, and pours
a flame through her yawning hoop,
a red nothing, one of everything.
And, with spite for tomorrow's sameness,
makes the wild river quiet inside.
With all her sex she turns away
from this possible unnatural temple

of transmogrified instants,
and throws a few gravestones
at her children, asleep in manicured
detachment, in an airplane that floats
like a song, in a Cadillac full
of roses (that stalls on the beach),
and on seahorses that back
into their twinkling caves;
an inclination to cling to them,
to not let them slip, to let them sleep —
an icicle that grows from a tree,
a feather thrown into a canyon,
a dime found in the snow.

MEADOW

First comes the wood-anemone
from the southernmost provinces
into the far north.
It covers the wooded pastures in spring
with its carpet of white gauze
before the foliage has yet grown thick enough
to offer shade.

The slender prune-cherry raises its network
of branches, veiled in white, airy
clusters of flowers that lavish
rich almond fragrance
to the light sky of the northern spring.

But soon the greenery is well under way in the groves,
and spring is already changing into summer
when the lily of the valley has its brief flowering,—

and so approaches the lavishly generous seasons
of the dog-rose, the butterly orchis,
that shy white gem of the dewy meadows
and damp wooded pastures,
how exotic it seems—

with its mysteriously formed flower spire
on a slim stalk
and its heavy Oriental fragrance . . .

No part of this flower may be reproduced
without permission in writing from the Creator.

WORKING CONDITIONS

Because you are the bridge for me
to cross over into myself,
you stand there in a curve of lace
holding white carnations,
your face shining in laughter
like a waterfall over my head.

I love you, I love you
full of wasps and spring air,
full of travels through stormy nights
in Balkan countries, taking the whole world
inside us; because we never learn,
because we stumble, we fall hard—

and the balance of chaos
has given us this chance
love dedicates its strife to us.

A BROKEN COWHAND

There's a road out there that ripples
over the horizon: an Oriental carpet
Gurdjieff, the imposter, wove
The moon is discovered to be almost human,
probably from hearing cowboy songs
on lonely nightwatch.
Hours go by, troop-carriers.
The body of the evening goes by in a tank.
Bambi, you had better be leaving now.

And everyone at the fire-station knows
that you are bonkers. Just as everyone
at the filling-station knows
that you're from Yonkers.
Everyone from Glenhaven knows,
knows their geography as well as
if not better than everybody from
Tompkins Cove. I return to the birthplace
of my rubber tree: I would sick chaos
on the unruly if for instance a citizen
of mine (1) took my broken heart for
a holiday, (2) violated my dog
before nightfall, (3) named
a child after me, Opening Valves.

DAY BOOK

811   Tate, James, 1943-
T
       Viper jazz

DATE			

2-77

Ⓡ THE BAKER & TAYLOR CO.